SUPPORTING LAGGING STUDENTS AND LEARNING FOR ALL
APPLYING THE DIAGNOSE-AND-SUPPLEMENT SYSTEM OF BASIC SKILLS IN THE REPUBLIC OF KOREA

Jae-Chun Ban, Sun Kim, and Meekyung Shin

FEBRUARY 2022

ASIAN DEVELOPMENT BANK

 Creative Commons Attribution 3.0 IGO license (CC BY 3.0 IGO)

© 2022 Asian Development Bank
6 ADB Avenue, Mandaluyong City, 1550 Metro Manila, Philippines
Tel +63 2 8632 4444; Fax +63 2 8636 2444
www.adb.org

Some rights reserved. Published in 2022.

ISBN 978-92-9269-304-6 (print); 978-92-9269-305-3 (electronic); 978-92-9269-306-0 (ebook)
Publication Stock No. SPR210528
DOI: http://dx.doi.org/10.22617/SPR210528

The views expressed in this publication are those of the authors and do not necessarily reflect the views and policies of the Asian Development Bank (ADB) or its Board of Governors or the governments they represent.

ADB does not guarantee the accuracy of the data included in this publication and accepts no responsibility for any consequence of their use. The mention of specific companies or products of manufacturers does not imply that they are endorsed or recommended by ADB in preference to others of a similar nature that are not mentioned.

By making any designation of or reference to a particular territory or geographic area, or by using the term "country" in this document, ADB does not intend to make any judgments as to the legal or other status of any territory or area.

This work is available under the Creative Commons Attribution 3.0 IGO license (CC BY 3.0 IGO) https://creativecommons.org/licenses/by/3.0/igo/. By using the content of this publication, you agree to be bound by the terms of this license. For attribution, translations, adaptations, and permissions, please read the provisions and terms of use at https://www.adb.org/terms-use#openaccess.

This CC license does not apply to non-ADB copyright materials in this publication. If the material is attributed to another source, please contact the copyright owner or publisher of that source for permission to reproduce it. ADB cannot be held liable for any claims that arise as a result of your use of the material.

Please contact pubsmarketing@adb.org if you have questions or comments with respect to content, or if you wish to obtain copyright permission for your intended use that does not fall within these terms, or for permission to use the ADB logo.

Corrigenda to ADB publications may be found at http://www.adb.org/publications/corrigenda.

Notes:
In this publication, "$" refers to United States dollars.
ADB recognizes "Korea" as the Republic of Korea.

On the cover: The Republic of Korea enables lagging students to catch up with their needed learning through the Diagnose-and-Supplement System of Basic Skills or DASOBS. This can be adapted to support and improve the quality of education in developing member countries of the Asian Development Bank (photos by ADB).

Contents

Tables and Figures	iv
Preface	v
Abbreviations	vi
Executive Summary	vii
I. Introduction	1
II. Purpose, Features, and Progress of the Diagnose-and-Supplement System of Basic Skills (DASOBS)	3
Impetus for DASOBS Development	3
Brief History of DASOBS Development	6
Policies to Support Lagging Students in the Republic of Korea	7
III. DASOBS Pipeline and Content	9
DASOBS Pipeline	9
DASOBS Components and Content	10
IV. DASOBS Operation	13
Essential Roles of DASOBS-Related Institutions	13
DASOBS Development Process and Operations	14
DASOBS Results	16
V. Implications for Policy Planning	19
References	21
About the Authors	22

Tables and Figures

Tables

1	Comparing NAEA and DASOBS	4
2	Outlining the Contents of DASOBS	11
3	The Contents of DASOBS by Grade	12
4	Number of Examinees for DTBS and Passing Rate (%)	16
5	Number of Schools that Conducted the DTBS in 2019	17
6	Number of Examinees and the Percentage of Those Passed in 2019 DTBS	18

Figures

1	History of DTBS Content Development	6
2	History of DASOBS Operation	7
3	BASECAMP Website	8
4	DASOBS Pipeline	9
5	Roles of DASOBS-Related Institutions	13
6	DASOBS Development Process	15
7	Percentage of Passing Students in DTBS, 2015–2019	17

Preface

Supporting lagging students is the foundation for ensuring learning for all. Students learn at different paces. Yet, some may struggle in one or more subjects and can fall behind quickly; as higher grade levels require them to learn more than the requirements in lower grade levels. For students with academic difficulties, this hierarchical nature of school can become a huge burden. The timely diagnosis of students' levels of academic achievement is crucial for managing an effective education system for this precise reason. To be considered high quality, the education system must identify exactly which students are likely to struggle or fail to meet the learning goals for the school year, and guide them with the appropriate support programs.

One of the ways to manage the quality of a class is to test the students' current state of learning. However, tests intended for the classroom may present problem-solving difficulties for some students, who may then simply guess the answers. Teachers, therefore, do not get the information on which parts of the curriculum these students struggle to grasp. A system must be established to provide such students with appropriate resources that will help them succeed in schools.

The Republic of Korea, in its first big step toward an education system that pays special attention to academically struggling students, has developed the Diagnose-and-Supplement System of Basic Skills (DASOBS) that identifies and provides extra support to students with academic abilities below the basic level. An initial diagnosis of all students determines which of them have above-basic abilities and which ones are below-basic learners. Supplemental learning material is then provided throughout the year to the below-basic group; the material can change as tests given during the year show progress among these students. The system is currently implemented for grades 1–10.

In introducing DASOBS, this report defines its purpose and characteristics along with a brief history of its development. It describes the system pipeline, content, and operations. Furthermore, the implications of implementing DASOBS in education policy are presented.

This report benefited from the personal guidance of Meekyung Shin, education specialist in the Education Sector Group, the Sustainable Development and Climate Change Department (SDCC), ADB who also served as a coauthor. Smita Gyawali, senior project officer, South Asia Department (SARD); Zhigang Li, senior social sector specialist, SARD; and Jukka Tulivuori, social sector specialist, SDCC, ADB provided valuable comments as peer reviewers. Me-an Asico, ADB consultant, edited the study report. Dorothy C. Geronimo, senior education officer, SDCC, coordinated the production. The development of this report, as a knowledge product, would not have been possible without the encouragement and overall guidance of Brajesh Panth, chief of the Education Sector Group, SDCC.

Abbreviations

AMEC	Applied Measurement & Evaluation Center
CCCL	Comprehensive Clinic Center of Learning
CNU	Chungnam National University
DASOBS	Diagnose-and-Supplement System of Basic Skills
DTBS	Diagnostic Test for Basic Skills
KERIS	Korea Education and Research Information Service
MOE	Ministry of Education
NAEA	National Assessment of Educational Achievement
OECD	Organisation for Economic Co-operation and Development
ROK	Republic of Korea

Executive Summary

Understanding students' abilities and skills relative to the demands of the curriculum and guiding them accordingly is a vital part of maintaining a high-quality education system. Students below the basic level of academic skills need more time to learn and more personalized guidance from their teachers. The Republic of Korea has been meeting this need by developing and running the Diagnose-and-Supplement System of Basic Skills (DASOBS). This system is used to guide academically underachieving students by diagnosing their basic academic abilities constantly and in stages, and providing them with supplemental material that matches their academics. This system is intended to raise the degree of attention paid by schools and teachers to students who are easily isolated from the rest of the class due to their lack of academic skills, and to improve students' quality of life by helping them experience academic success over and over again.

The ultimate purpose of DASOBS is to give academically underachieving students the attention they need, in a world that tends to focus more on students who excel. Major features of this system include using tests that can precisely identify academically struggling students, testing below-basic students regularly throughout the school year to track their progress, and providing them with personalized guidance suited to the academic needs of each student.

DASOBS testing is done more than once in the year. The first Diagnostic Test for Basic Skills (DTBS) is administered at the start of the year, and other diagnostic tests are carried out in three stages during the year. Only those students who placed below-basic in the initial diagnostic test take the succeeding tests. After each test, the students are provided with supplemental material in the subject areas they struggled with in the test. The test type the students take the next time depends on how they performed in the previous DTBS. Different test types cover different ranges of content. Below-basic students are thus grouped into smaller and more specific subgroups after each test, and provided with more personalized academic support.

Many institutions, each one with a specific role, take part in DASOBS. Without their efficient cooperation, DASOBS cannot achieve its objectives. The Applied Measurement & Evaluation Center (AMEC) at Chungnam National University (CNU), is the main developer of DASOBS content on top of its many other responsibilities. AMEC forms various teams to develop, review, and revise test items, and eventually create supplemental learning material corresponding to the finalized test items. This material is then uploaded to the database so that it can be used online or offline by schools. Not all schools in the Republic of Korea use DASOBS, as it is not mandatory; however, about half of all schools in the country use the system.

DASOBS has numerous policy implications. It enables students to be monitored, teachers to be equipped to provide students with the specific academic support they need, and the related institutions to be organized. Moreover, implementing an online system is very closely aligned with today's world, especially in light of the coronavirus disease (COVID-19) pandemic. The goal of DASOBS was to create an educational environment that gives all students equal opportunities to succeed—a place where meaningful learning happens even among the lowest-achieving students. Again, supporting lagging students is the foundation for ensuring learning for all.

I. Introduction

Citizens have the right to learn the skills needed to live in a society through school education. For a country, educating its people to equip them with those basic skills is an equally important duty. The Republic of Korea (ROK) has put considerable effort into making sure that all students obtain at least the minimum skills required for this heavily knowledge-based society before diving into the real world.

Basic scholastic skills for all students are addressed by many government policies (MOE 2019). Among other policy measures, the government planned and implemented the Zero Plan for students with below-basic scholastic ability, opened the Center for Comprehensive Learning Clinic in 2012. Since 2014, it has been operating Do-Dream Schools, which specialize in education for struggling learners who are unmotivated to learn, are emotionally unstable, have behavioral problems, come from a multicultural background, or have difficulty learning for other reasons (MOE 2016). Broadly speaking, therefore, the government has presented a set of plans giving definite form to its support for below-basic students (MOE 2019), and it has been reinforcing its administrative functions.

To ensure that students without basic academic skills acquire the minimum scholastic abilities before advancing to the next grade, the most important task is to check, first, which students, if any, are falling behind in some subjects, and to provide those students with guidance that matches their level. This checking should start early in elementary school, as students at higher grade obtain material that ultimately requires understanding of material from the previous year. Students must complete the expected material for their respective grades, as verified by the educators, to reach the minimum level of achievement for each grade or subject.

Each student has unique academic abilities and absorbs material at a different pace. The academic performance of students should therefore be evaluated based on accurate and objective data. Students must be guided with detailed and personalized plans for each content area of a subject. The Organisation for Economic Co-operation and Development (OECD) conducted research studies on students with low academic achievements and recommended that an educational support system for students must be implemented as early as possible (OECD 2016, p. 196). According to the OECD, students with low academic achievement in two or more subjects have to be identified, and a policy focusing educators' attention on these students should be in place. In 2016–2018, according to data analysis by Kim et al. (2020), 48.6% of the students who did not reach the minimum academic level in at least one subject in grades 3–6 did not make the cut in two or more subjects.

In the ROK, the Diagnose-and-Supplement System of Basic Skills system (DASOBS) has been developed and disseminated to the frontline school system at the national level to enable educators to determine students' basic academic abilities systematically and provide each student with appropriate learning tools. DASOBS has three main tasks. It first checks students who are starting a new grade and identifies those who are below the basic academic level. Then it checks the progress of below-basic students at regular intervals throughout the year to detect improvements in their basic academic abilities. Finally, after each diagnosis, it provides supplemental learning material related to each testing question to students without the basic scholastic abilities. This system is currently being used in grades 1–10.

There are concerns that the ability gap among students is widening as students attend online classes rather than going to school in person due to the coronavirus disease (COVID-19) pandemic. In this situation, a system should be put in place, which continuously diagnoses and corrects students lacking basic academic abilities.

This knowledge product introduces DASOBS as it is being used in the ROK—to describe how it operates and provide insights on the system's policy implications.

II. Purpose, Features, and Progress of the Diagnose-and-Supplement System of Basic Skills (DASOBS)

Impetus for DASOBS Development

DASOBS was developed to help academically underachieving students who are easily isolated from the school system. By paying more attention to those students from schools and teachers, and providing them with personalized diagnostic and supplemental guidance, the system strives to create repeated instances of academic success, thus making their school experience more meaningful. More specifically, DASOBS development was driven by several objectives.

First, this system was developed to support the educational welfare of academic underachievers or academically underachieving students. As all students in a class are equally important, the pace of the class should ideally match the learning pace of all the students. However, because each student is different, the pace tends to match the average learning speed. Those without basic academic abilities are easily isolated, and after falling behind repeatedly, can lose motivation to learn, confidence, and positive self-image. DASOBS tries to prevent this from happening by regularly identifying underachieving students and creating learning environments that match their academic setting.

Second, the system is intended to provide insights into improvements during the school year in the basic academic skills of underachieving students. It implements a recurring, step-by-step diagnose–supplement–re-diagnose–supplement process to manage these students throughout the period. This process continually examines the progress made by students in specific areas of the curriculum within the year and gives them suitable guidance; in this way, it differs from once-a-year testing for the general student body.

Third, by distributing standardized assessment tools reflecting the national-level curriculum, DASOBS is designed to measure the strengths and weaknesses of students in each subject according to a unified national standard.

Fourth, the system is able to assess whether the learning abilities of students have reached the basic level by including test items suited to their target academic setting. Tests conducted by schoolteachers typically consist of hard, medium, and easy problems, of which hard and medium problems are often too difficult for students below the basic academic level, who consequently attempt to solve only a few problems. As a result, DASOBS deals with the specific areas of struggle in underachieving students, the data which schools lack.

Fifth, traditional textbooks have too much content and are generally too challenging for academically underachieving students. The supplemental learning material in DASOBS, based on curriculum achievement standards, accommodates these students and their needs. Teachers are also provided with useful tools to enhance the learning of below-basic students, instead of being encumbered by the time-consuming and arduous task of making this supplemental material themselves.

Sixth, the system takes a unified national approach to setting an objective basis for deciding whether students meet the basic academic standards, thus speeding up the diagnostic process, and making it more objective and fair. Teachers, who no longer having to do the assessment themselves, can focus on guiding below-basic students.

Features of DASOBS

In the ROK, DASOBS and the National Assessment of Educational Achievement (NAEA) are national-level assessment systems that measure the general degree of academic achievement in students. The NAEA analyzes changes in the level of curriculum achievement by sampling around 3%–5% of the students in grades 9 and 10 (Ra, Kim, and Rhee 2019). Students are tested once a year and classified into advanced, proficient, basic, and below-basic achievement levels. The grade-9 test uses material from grade 7 to the first semester of grade 9; however, it is generally beyond the capabilities of below-basic students. Determining precisely which material from which grades and subjects presents learning difficulties for below-basic students is far from easy.

DASOBS, however, is targeted at students in grades 1–10 and provides valuable information about whether they have the basic academic abilities to complete the curriculum for their current grade. The test itself, which repeatedly assesses the academic performance of students, is undemanding, and the results provide detailed and exact information about the knowledge deficiencies of below-basic students. A comparison of the two systems is shown in **Table 1**.

Table 1: Comparing NAEA and DASOBS

Item	NAEA	DASOBS
Purpose	To provide information that can be referenced to enhance curriculum achievement and improve curriculum quality by examining national trends in academic achievement levels	To support academically underachieving students in gradually obtaining basic learning abilities by continuously evaluating the students and providing them with supplemental guidance throughout the school year
Targets	Grades 9 and 11 Sample schools around 3%–5%	Grades 1–10 Start of the semester: all students Throughout the semester: students who placed below-basic on the initial diagnostic test
Subjects	**Grade 9**: Korean, social studies, math, natural science, and English **Grade 10**: Korean, math, and English	**Grades 1 and 2**: basic Korean and basic math **Grade 3**: reading, writing, and arithmetic **Grades 4–9**: Korean, social studies, history, math, natural science, and English **Grade 10**: Korean, math, and English
Test period	September	March, June, September, and December
Material covered	**Grade 9**: Grades 7–9 (first semester) **Grade 10**: Korean, English: cross-curricular material **Grade 10 math**: high school math	**Grades 1, 2**: curriculum material for grades 1 and 2 **Grade 3**: curriculum material for grades 1–3 **Grades 4–10**: material from the previous year to the current year
Assessed achievement levels	Below-basic, basic, proficient, and advanced	Below-basic and above-basic
Levels of difficulty	Level 1 to Level 4	Curriculum fulfillment level "low"

DASOBS = Diagnose-and-Supplement System of Basic Skills, NAEA = National Assessment of Educational Achievement.
Source: Authors.

DASOBS has several noteworthy features:

First, it consists of the initial diagnostic test, the Diagnostic Test for Basic Skills (DTBS), and supplemental learning material.

Second, it is a level-based, stick-to-the-curriculum system for academically underachieving students. There are three different types of DTBS. A student who passes one type of test can move on to the next one. However, a student who fails one type of test must take another test of the same type after a certain period of supplemental learning. The test types do not vary in difficulty but differ only in the material covered, providing insights into how the basic academic skills of students progress during the year.

Third, the test content is up-to-date and kept abreast of the most recent curriculum, allowing its use by teachers as a student's guide in line with the national-level curriculum.

Fourth, all test questions are at the lowest level of national curriculum fulfillment standards, making them particularly easy. In fact, average scores on the 2019 DASOBS test ranged from 76% to 93%.

Fifth, all items in all tests, and the supplemental material known as *Nulpumi*,[1] are directly related. For instance, all the important concepts and practice problems for problem 1 in the grade 10 math test are included in *Nulpumi*. This means that if a student gets the problem wrong, he or she can easily go to the supplemental material, review the concepts, and solve practice problems. The student can then solve another problem correctly measuring the same material as problem 1.

Sixth, this system uses the Bookmark standard-setting method (Cizek 2012), rather than a norm-referenced method, to set standards consistent with the national-level curriculum. The system can, therefore, diagnose students objectively regardless of where they go to school.

Seventh, to allow teachers to focus mainly on guiding their academically underachieving students, a university and a government-funded research institution collaborate on the development and delivery of the tests, the test results, and the supplemental material.

Eighth, the system is flexible: all things can be performed either online or offline. Schools can thus make decisions depending on their situation. For example, all students must take the initial diagnostic test in March; however, bigger schools most likely do not have computer laboratories big enough to accommodate all students for testing. These schools may decide to have the test done offline instead, and simply print and distribute paper copies of the test to students. Smaller schools, on the contrary, can fit all students into their computer laboratories and can carry out the test, and also get the results online.

Ninth, while creating all the test items and supplemental material, the system focuses on below-basic students, and is well placed to identify and guide them.

Tenth, as the system covers grades 1–10, testing students regularly and providing them with the necessary support will prevent knowledge deficiencies in basic academic skills from accumulating over several years.

---

[1] A Korean term for a person with good potential for improvement.

Brief History of DASOBS Development

Both the diagnostic test and the DTBS are now part of DASOBS; however, these were developed separately. The diagnostic test was developed in 2008–2011 under the supervision of a metropolitan or provincial office of education. The rest of most offices of education throughout the country provided funding support for the development of the test and utilized it. Even the cut scores on the diagnostic test were based on sample data from that office alone, and test scores were not psychometrically comparable. The percentage of below-basic students fluctuated from year to year. It is unclear whether the percentage differences between years were due to the yearly changes of test difficulty or due to changes in students' abilities. In 2008–2011, the diagnostic test was administered only to students in grades 3–5 and 7–8.

DTBS was proposed by Chungnam National University (CNU) in 2009 and was first implemented, also in 2009, with financial support from the Daejeon Metropolitan Office of Education.

DTBS was developed only for grade 4 in 2009; however, it was later expanded to cover upper grades, eventually including grades 5 and 6 by 2011, grades 7 and 8 by 2012, grade 9 by 2013, and grade 10 by 2018. Through test equating, CNU, AMEC maintained the consistency of DTBS cut scores over the years. However until 2011, there was no apparent psychometric relationship between the diagnostic test and DTBS as these tests were developed by different institutions.

In 2012, however, as CNU took charge of developing both the diagnostic test and DTBS, the psychometric relationship between the two started to take shape. The term "DASOBS" was first used in 2015, and AMEC at CNU is currently developing the entire system and disseminating it throughout the country (**Figures 1** and **2**).

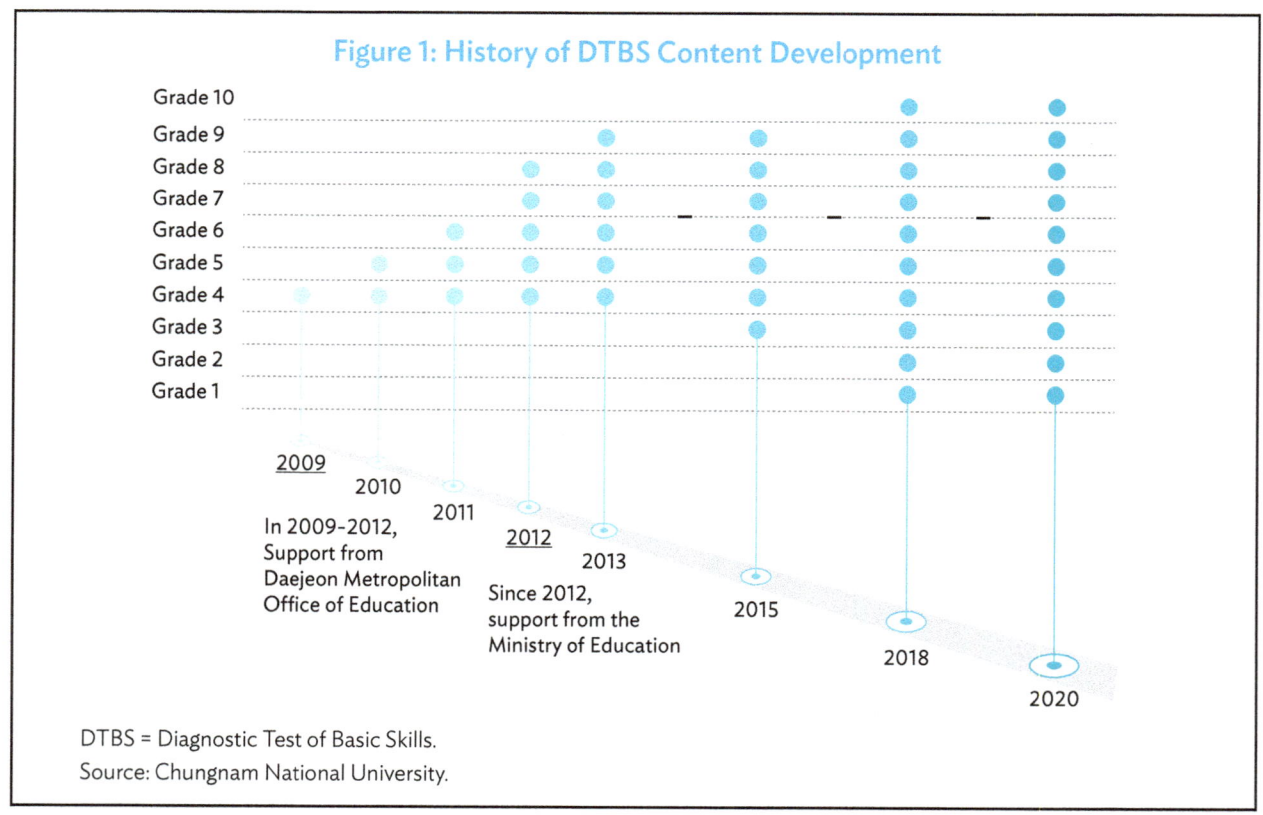

Figure 1: History of DTBS Content Development

DTBS = Diagnostic Test of Basic Skills.
Source: Chungnam National University.

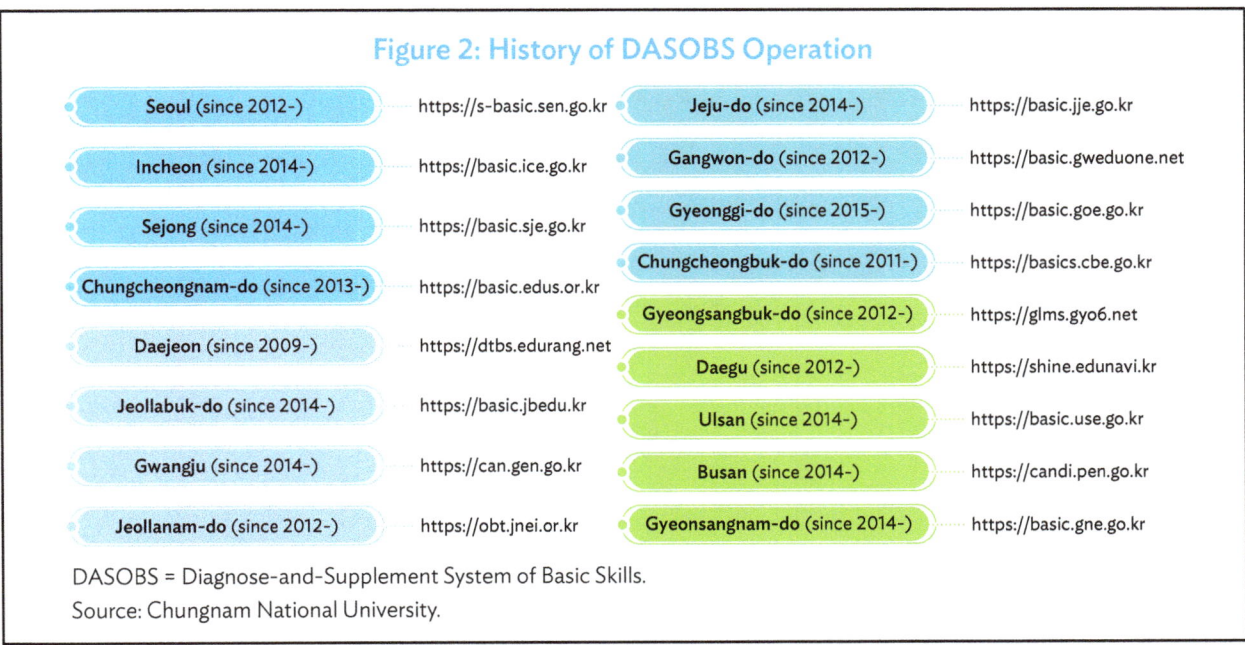

Figure 2: History of DASOBS Operation

DASOBS = Diagnose-and-Supplement System of Basic Skills.
Source: Chungnam National University.

In 2020, DASOBS content was provided to all schools in the ROK for grades 1–10, and DASOBS tools are used by all 17 metropolitan and provincial offices of education. Korean schools overseas and even nonschool institutions supporting child learning can also request for DASOBS material.

In March 2020, a website called BASECAMP was launched. Whereas DASOBS focuses on regular diagnostic tests implemented by schools, BASECAMP, by storing all released DASOBS content in a database, allows students to learn material freely from any specific grade and subject, and at any time. They can choose the content that they wish to supplement and can use this to master certain subject areas. Especially during this COVID-19 pandemic, BASECAMP ensures that students who cannot be physically present in school can resume learning and achieve the basic level of academic skills. DASOBS is the only system in the ROK to reach such a high degree of comprehensiveness and scientific rigor in the diagnosis and supplementation of basic scholastic ability.

Policies to Support Lagging Students in the Republic of Korea

In addition to DASOBS, various policy measures are used in the ROK to support lagging students. Three of these policy measures are cited here. The first one is Do-Dream School that has been running since 2014; it implements a policy to comprehensively support students who have difficulty in learning due to complex factors. Do-Dream School diagnose the causes of low academic achievement and provide students with learning coaching and counseling services within the school. Second is the Comprehensive Clinic Center of Learning (CCCL), which is operated in accordance with a policy to provide customized help from experts from outside of school, to students who are struggling with their studies due to cognitive, emotional, and behavioral factors. Students who show academic maladjustment due to psychological causes are given the emotional support through professional counseling. If the accumulation of learning deficits is severe, CCCL provides students with the program for improving learning motivation and coaching learning strategies. The third involves various support programs for students with multicultural backgrounds. Multicultural students are not familiar with the Korean culture and often suffer from low achievement due to language barriers. For these students, the ROK provides programs for Korean language education and counseling services.

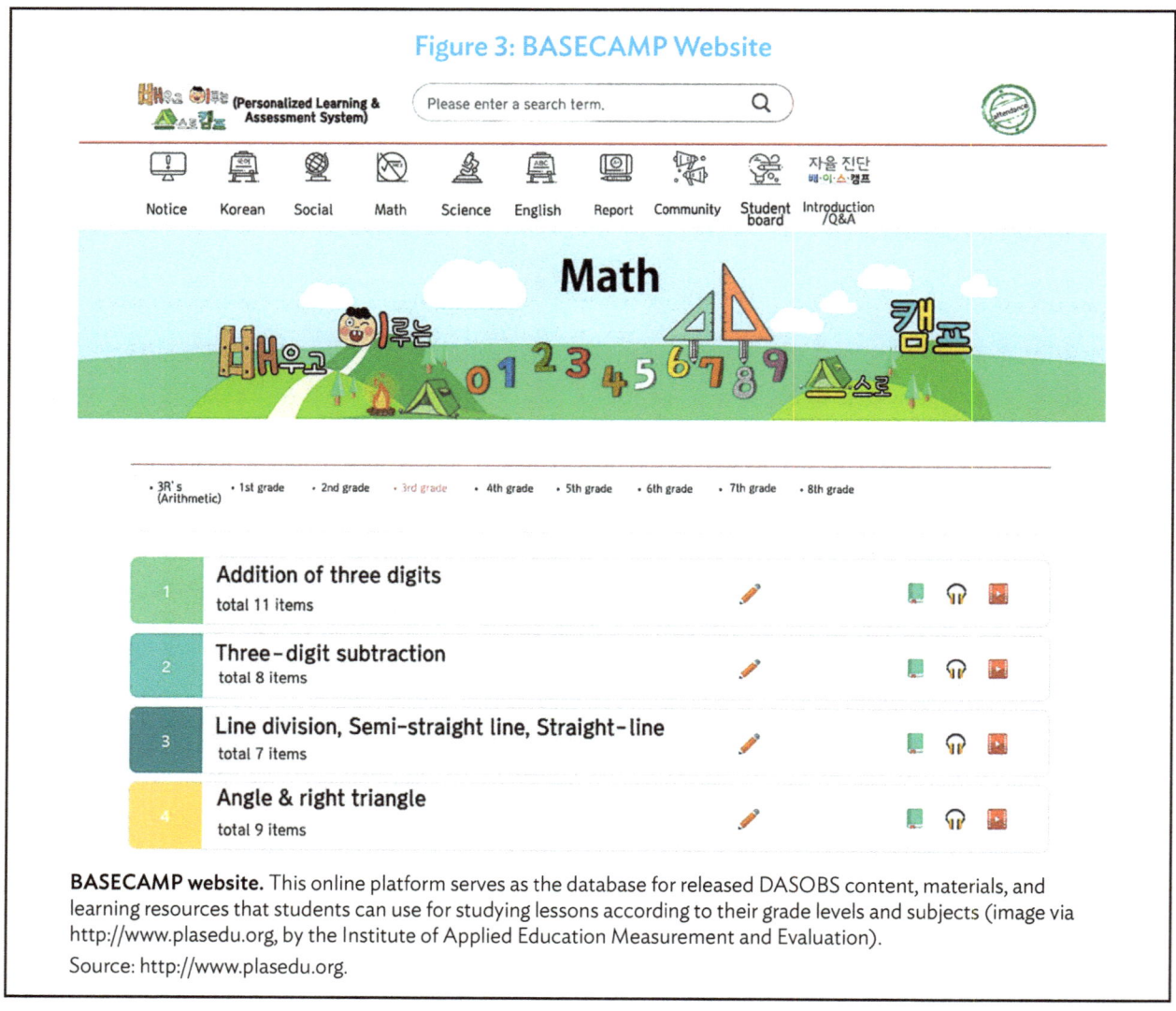

Figure 3: BASECAMP Website

BASECAMP website. This online platform serves as the database for released DASOBS content, materials, and learning resources that students can use for studying lessons according to their grade levels and subjects (image via http://www.plasedu.org, by the Institute of Applied Education Measurement and Evaluation).

Source: http://www.plasedu.org.

III. DASOBS Pipeline and Content

DASOBS Pipeline

Based on the DASOBS pipeline, shown in **Figure 4**, the diagnostic test takes place at the start of the school year in March. All the sample schools carry out the test on a set date early in the month, and the rest of the schools choose their test dates and hold the test online or offline. However, schools that complete the test sooner cannot release the test items online or on other media. To be under DASOBS management, students must place below-basic in the diagnostic test or be endorsed for testing by their teachers. The subjects in which they place below-basic can vary between students, and number between one and five. The teacher has to register the students online along with the specified subjects. They are then provided with supplemental guidance through *Nulpumi* over a certain period. Schools also have their own programs to help these students.

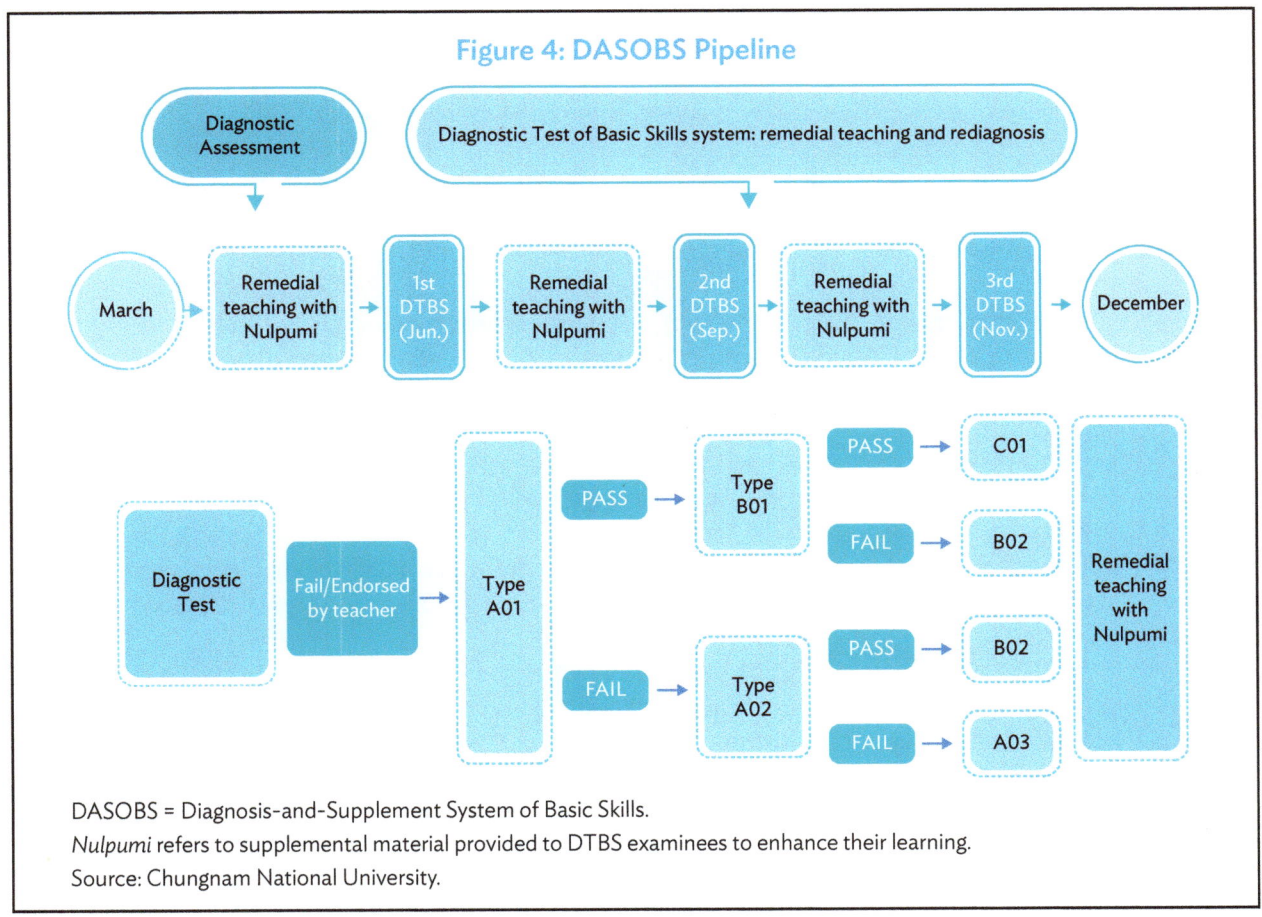

Figure 4: DASOBS Pipeline

DASOBS = Diagnosis-and-Supplement System of Basic Skills.
Nulpumi refers to supplemental material provided to DTBS examinees to enhance their learning.
Source: Chungnam National University.

The first DTBS is given sometime in June; the exact date depends on each school's schedule. All students registered in DASOBS take the A01 test and are again classified as above- or below-basic. This test covers the same material as the diagnostic test, so, by implication, a student who passes the A01 test has the basic academic abilities needed for the previous grade. After the test, material related to incorrectly answered questions is automatically extracted from *Nulpumi* for each student; however, the full version can be downloaded by students who wish to do so. This supplemental material can then be used in schools to enhance the students' learning.

The second DTBS is held sometime in September, on a date that also depends on each school's schedule. Students who passed the A01 test take the B01 test; those who failed the first test take A02, another form of A01. Supplemental learning material is similarly provided to students who need it.

The third DTBS is carried out in the same way as the first and second tests, sometime in December. Those who passed B01 take C01, and those who failed B01 take B02. Those who took A02 in the second DTBS now take B02 if they passed A02, and A03 if they did not. DASOBS takes into account the variations in pace at which students learn and evaluates their skills with proper tools, depending on how they performed their previous test. Students can thus be provided with supplemental learning in their specific areas of difficulty.

DASOBS Components and Content

DASOBS contains various diagnostic assessment tests and supplemental material for below-basic students in grades 1–10. At the core of the diagnostic portion are the diagnostic test and DTBS. These two can be used for grades 3–10, and as their main purpose is to measure basic scholastic abilities, most of the test items are multiple-choice questions. The subjects these tests cover may vary depending on the grade; however, Korean, math, social studies, natural science, and English are usually included. **Table 2** shows the content of DASOBS.

Students from grades 1 and 2 are too young to take written tests. Therefore, after the first semester of the first grade, teachers use the diagnostic tools for basic Korean and basic math to find out whether students properly grasped what they were taught, and provide them with supplemental material if needed.

The tests for the 3Rs (reading, writing, and arithmetic) are mainly for third graders, but are available even for higher grades in a separate form (*Sooksook,* meaning growing up steadily, 1, 2) in case these students still struggle in any of the three components.

Test results showing whether students have the basic academic skills are reported; however, teachers may also want to know where the learning deficiencies of students begin. For this purpose, there are detailed subject-specific diagnostic tools for grades 1–6. A sixth grader who placed below-basic in math, for example, can be sequentially tested with this set of tools based on curriculum material from grades 1 to 6 to pinpoint exactly which concept in which the subject and grade poses the first learning difficulties for this particular student.

Nulpumi, the DASOBS supplemental material, has the content that relates directly back to the test items. It summarizes the key concepts needed to solve the test questions and provides plenty of practice problems to make sure that these concepts are understood by students. *Nulpumi* is specifically designed to allow students who incorrectly answer questions on the diagnostic test or DTBS to simply go back to *Nulpumi* to understand the concepts behind each incorrectly answered question. The system also provides extra material related to basic English, reading, and other subjects, regardless of the grade.

Table 2: Outlining the Contents of DASOBS

Item	Content
Target grades	• Elementary and school: grades 1–6 • Middle school: grades 7–9 • High school: grade 10
Target students	• Diagnostic test: all students or those endorsed for testing by teachers • DTBS: those who placed below-basic on the diagnostic test or were endorsed by their teachers
Subjects covered	• Grades 1 and 2: basic Korean, and basic math • 3Rs: reading, writing, and arithmetic • Diagnostic test: Korean, social studies (history), math, natural science, and English (for grade 10, only Korean, math, and English) • DTBS: Korean, social studies (history), math, natural science, and English (for grade 10, only Korean, math, and English)
Test types	• Basic Korean and basic math (three types) • 3Rs (four types) • Basic English (the alphabet): types A and B (same material for both types) • Diagnostic test: types G and H • DTBS: types A, B, and C • Diagnostic material for subareas: Korean • Diagnostic material for subareas: math
Material covered	• Basic Korean: first semester of grade 1 • Basic math: grades 1 and 2 • 3Rs: *Tantan* 1, 2 (grades 1–2 curricula); *Sooksook* 1, 2 (grades 1–2 curricula) • Basic English: grade 2 • Diagnostic test, type A: previous year • Type B: second semester of previous year up to first semester of current year • Type C: current year up to the second week of November • Diagnostic material for subareas: grades 1–6
Number of items	• Basic Korean, basic math: 10–15 activity-type items • 3Rs: 25 short-answer and multiple-choice questions • Grades 4–6: 25 multiple-choice questions • Grades 7–10: 30 multiple-choice questions
Timeline	• Diagnostic test: sometime in March (schools may choose the date) • DTBS: type A in June, type B in September, and type C in December (schools may choose the dates within those periods) • Diagnostic material for subareas: classes may choose the material.
Operation methods	• Grades 1 and 2: teachers use diagnostic activity tools to check whether students can solve problems. • Grades 3–10: operate either online or offline. - Each metropolitan or provincial office of education has a DASOBS website.

Supplemental material
 	
Guidance material
	• Necessary concepts and practice problems for each test item
	  - Grades 1–2: basic Korean and basic math
	  - Grade 3: 3Rs (reading, writing, and arithmetic)
	  - Grades 4–6: Korean, social studies, math, natural science, and English
	  - Preparatory English for middle school
	  - Grades 7–9: Korean, social science, Social Science 1, Social Science 2, History 1, History 2, math, natural science, and English
	  - Grade 10: Korean, math, and English
	• Nongraded system material
	  - Step-by-step Korean reading
	  - Step-by-step math
	  - English alphabet material
	• Basic learning material: English Phonics 1 and 2
	• Reading fluency application "*Hangul* Treasure Hunt" (developed and distributed for Android and iOS)

DASOBS = Diagnose-and-Supplement System of Basic Skills, DTBS = Diagnostic Test for Basic Skills, *Tantan* means growing up firmly in Korean, *Sooksook* means growing up steadily.

Source: Authors' work based on Chungnam National University, DASOBS.

There are three types of DTBS. Type A (A01, A02, and A03) covers the previous year's curriculum; Type B (B01 and B02) deals with material from the second semester of the previous year up to the first semester of the current year, and Type C (C01), with material for the current year up to mid-November. DTBS testing, with different ranges of material, is done throughout the year because passing the type A test in March demonstrates only that the student has reached the basic level of academic skills for the previous grade, and nothing more. However, passing the type C test implies that the student has the basic academic skills needed not only for the previous grade but also for the current grade. **Table 3** summarizes the DASOBS content by grade.

Table 3: The Contents of DASOBS by Grade

Contents		1	2	3	4	5	6	7	8	9	10
3Rs	Development	-	-	•	•	•	•	•	•	•	•
	Area	-	-	Reading, writing, arithmetic				Reading, writing, number and arithmetic			Reading, writing, understanding and use of arithmetic
Diagnostic tests	Development	•	•	•	•	•	•	•	•	•	•
	Subject	Basic Korean, basic math		Korean, social science, math, science, and English							Korean, math, and English
Diagnostic material for subareas	Development	•	•	•	•	•	•	-	-	-	-
	Area	Reading, writing, number and computation, data and probability, measurement, geometry, and regularity						-			-
DTBS	Development	-	-	-	•	•	•	•	•	•	•
	Area	-	-	-	Korean, social science, history, math, science, and English						Korean, math, and English
Supplemental material	Development	•	•	•	•	•	•	•	•	•	•
	Area	-		Reading, writing, and arithmetic				Reading, writing, number and arithmetic			Reading, writing, understanding, and use of arithmetic
				Step-by-step Korean reading, step-by-step math, English alphabet material, English phonics 1, 2				Math and science material for subareas			
	Subject	Basic Korean and basic math		-		Korean, social science, history, math, science, and English					Korean, math, and English

DASOBS = Diagnose-and-Supplement System of Basic Skills, DTBS = Diagnostic Test for Basic Skills, • under service, - = not applicable.
Source: Authors' work based on Chungnam National University, DASOBS.

IV. DASOBS Operation

Essential Roles of DASOBS-Related Institutions

Various institutions collaborate to run DASOBS. The main ones include the Ministry of Education (MOE), the 17 metropolitan and provincial offices of education, AMEC, the Korea Education and Research Information Service (KERIS), the Korea Institute for Curriculum and Evaluation (KICE), and the schools. Each institution has its own role, as shown in **Figure 5**, and it communicates and meets constantly with other institutions for the smooth running of DASOBS.

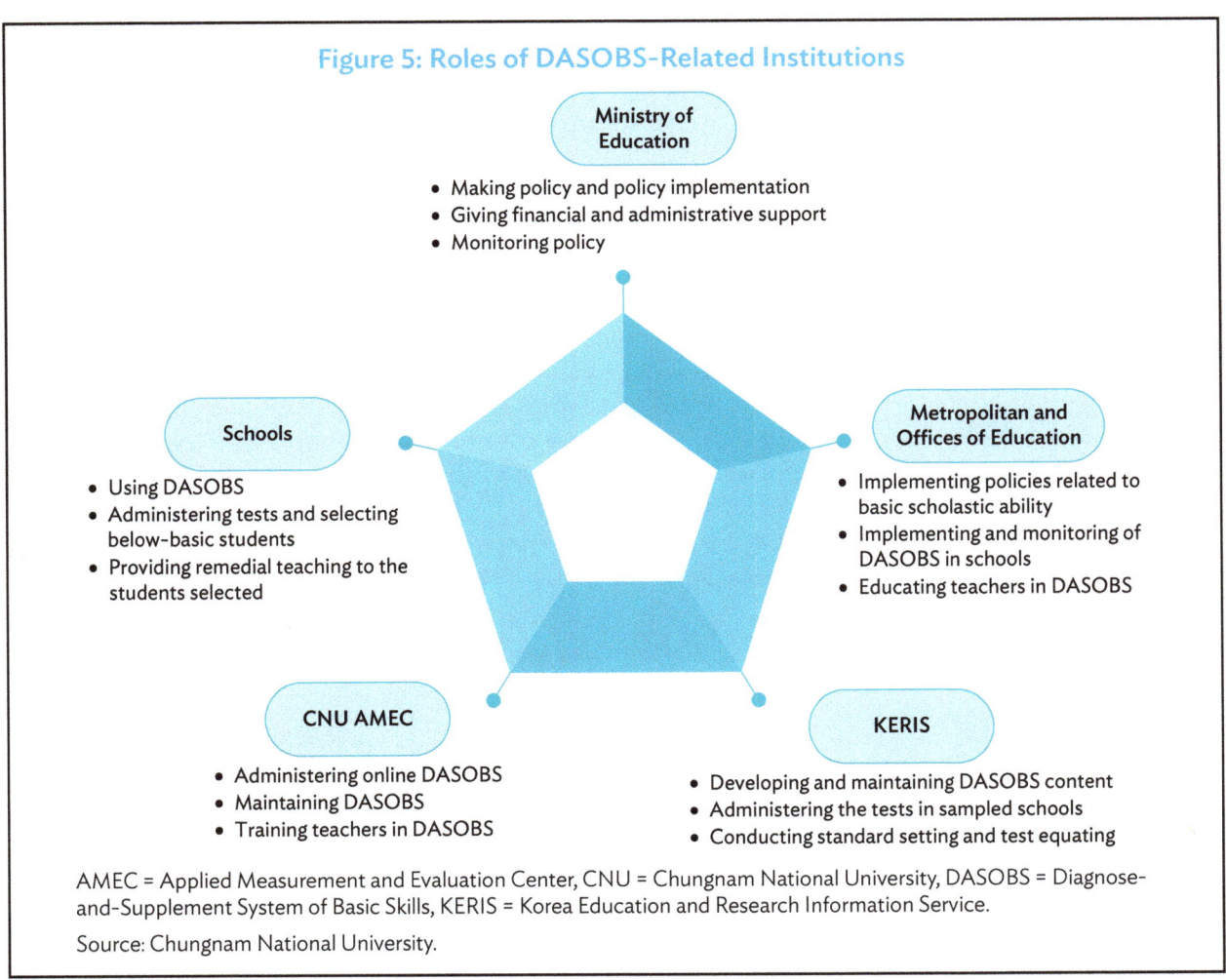

Figure 5: Roles of DASOBS-Related Institutions

Ministry of Education
- Making policy and policy implementation
- Giving financial and administrative support
- Monitoring policy

Schools
- Using DASOBS
- Administering tests and selecting below-basic students
- Providing remedial teaching to the students selected

Metropolitan and Offices of Education
- Implementing policies related to basic scholastic ability
- Implementing and monitoring of DASOBS in schools
- Educating teachers in DASOBS

CNU AMEC
- Administering online DASOBS
- Maintaining DASOBS
- Training teachers in DASOBS

KERIS
- Developing and maintaining DASOBS content
- Administering the tests in sampled schools
- Conducting standard setting and test equating

AMEC = Applied Measurement and Evaluation Center, CNU = Chungnam National University, DASOBS = Diagnose-and-Supplement System of Basic Skills, KERIS = Korea Education and Research Information Service.
Source: Chungnam National University.

The MOE, which supervises all the related institutions and monitors the whole operation, establishes work plans and provides financial support. It resolves differences of opinion and has the final say on important agendas. All the expenses of the system are covered by the ministry; DASOBS can, therefore, be used by schools and students at no cost to them.

The 17 metropolitan and provincial offices of education cooperate in developing the DASOBS content, establishing and implementing their own policies for defining and developing basic scholastic ability, and giving administrative support to schools to ensure that they use DASOBS correctly. They train teachers to use DASOBS, select teachers to review items that are developed, and form a panel to set standards for passing the tests and send the list of teachers chosen for the panel to AMEC.

Besides developing all content in DASOBS, AMEC takes charge of administering the tests in sample schools nationwide. It also conducts test equating, standard setting, online database construction and management, teacher training, and BASECAMP website (http://www.plasedu.org) operation.

KERIS administers the online DASOBS tests, maintains the DASOBS content, and trains teachers to use the system. It runs a call center to identify and resolve issues raised by users.

Schools use DASOBS to test students and group together those who place below-basic. They also take the responsibility for guiding these students and monitoring their progress.

DASOBS Development Process and Operations

DASOBS content is developed by about 900 people, which include current teachers in elementary, middle, and high schools; subject matter professors; educational measurement and evaluation experts; and others. **Figure 6** summarizes the DASOBS development process.

- **Developing the test items and supplemental material.** AMEC forms item development, item review, supplemental material development, and illustration or graphic teams to develop the content for all three parts of DASOBS. The test item and supplemental material teams include teachers who majored in the subject they will work on as part of those teams. The item development team analyzes the curriculum standards for each grade and selects educational achievement standards that can be measured on paper. Then for each subject, the team develops test items that reflect the minimum achievement level for a given achievement standard. The item review team then reviews these test items and gives feedback to the item development team to guide the latter in revising the test items. The illustration or graphic team is in charge of creating illustrations and graphics included in the tests and supplemental material. After all the test items are developed, and the supplemental material development team develops supplemental material linked with the test items.

- **Incorporating the test items and supplemental material into a database.** Once the test items and supplemental material are finalized, they are incorporated into a database and are used in online tests (There are as yet no statistical data on the use of these test items.)

- **Administering the diagnostic test.** School sampling is done using the proportional stratified cluster method. The sample schools, once selected, conduct the diagnostic test on a specific date in early March. AMEC sends the paper version of the tests to the sample schools, and the schools send back the optical mark recognition (OMR) sheets after the tests are completed. Sample students in each grade number range from 5,300 to 6,150, or constitute about 1.2%–1.4% of all students in each grade (grades 3–9). Those in grades 1 and 2 are too young to take tests on paper, as pointed out earlier, and grade 10 students already have to take far too many tests, so they are excluded from sampling.

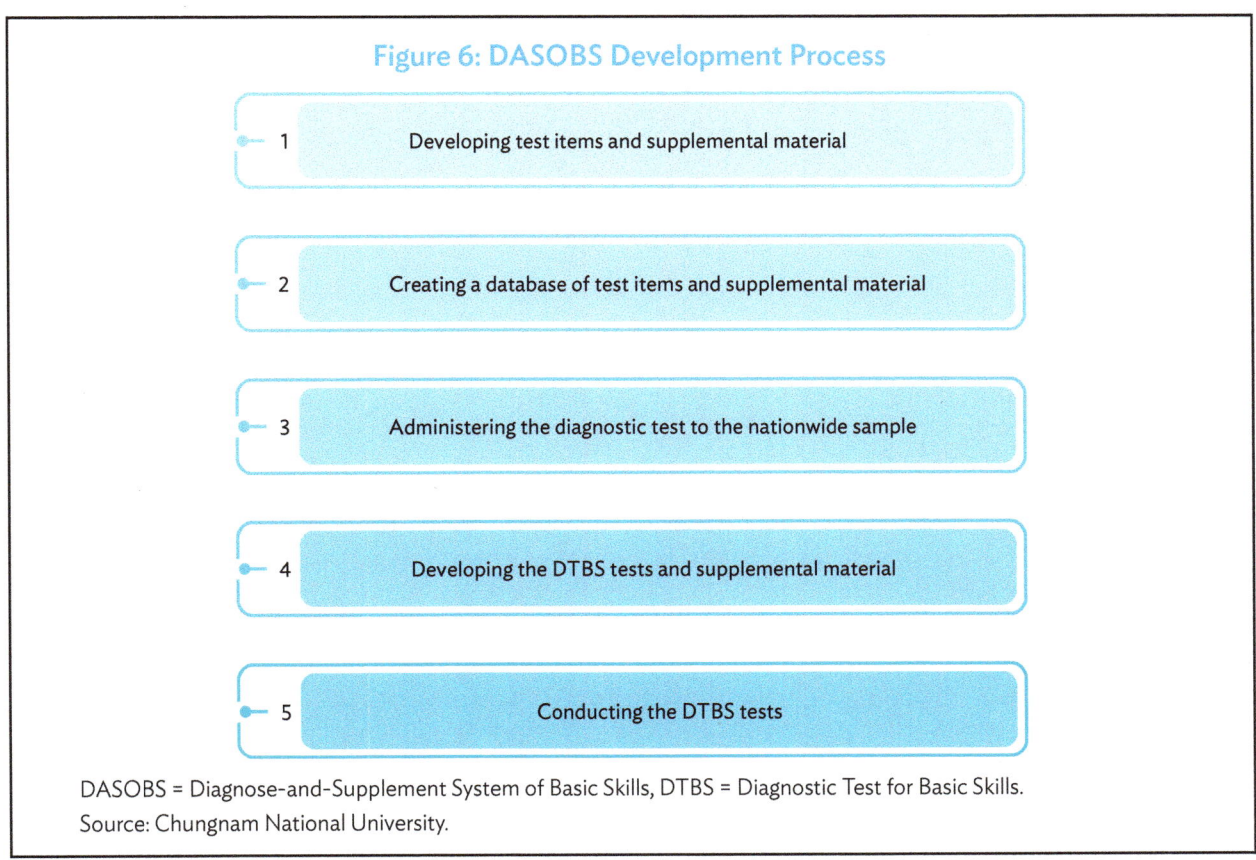

Figure 6: DASOBS Development Process

1. Developing test items and supplemental material
2. Creating a database of test items and supplemental material
3. Administering the diagnostic test to the nationwide sample
4. Developing the DTBS tests and supplemental material
5. Conducting the DTBS tests

DASOBS = Diagnose-and-Supplement System of Basic Skills, DTBS = Diagnostic Test for Basic Skills.
Source: Chungnam National University.

AMEC decodes the OMR sheets and analyzes each item statistically and psychometrically. With the resulting data, AMEC sets cut scores using the Bookmark standard-setting method (Mitzel et al. 2001) to separate the above-basic students from the rest of those taking the test, and determines whether the percentage of above-basic students has increased appreciably over the years, outpacing the change in the percentage of below-basic students. Once the cut scores for each subject are finalized, the item response theory (IRT) true-score equating method (Baker and Kim 2004) is used to equate the different test types or forms so that the test scores are comparable (Kolen and Brennan 2014). This way, no matter which test types or forms the students take, they can still place either above- or below-basic according to the same standard. Within 2 weeks after the diagnostic test, the cut scores for each subject are released to schools and are also uploaded to the database when the scoring software is distributed to the schools.

As soon as the cut scores are uploaded to the database, students who took the test online will know whether they placed above- or below-basic. The sample schools, which always carry out the test before this upload date of the cut scores, will be able to provide their students with their test results only after uploading to the database. Students who take the test online will be given supplemental learning booklets with the content related to the questions they answered incorrectly, and will thus get personalized supplemental material quickly. As mentioned earlier, they can always obtain *Nulpumi* in its entirety if they so wish.

After the diagnostic test, done either online or offline, below-basic students are registered in DASOBS. They then take the three DTBS tests at spaced intervals during the year and get supplemental material accordingly.

- **Developing the DTBS test items and the supplemental material.** The DTBS test items are developed separately for each subject, following a process that is very similar to the development of the diagnostic test. The main difference is that the diagnostic test has only two types, while DTBS has three types (A, B, and C). The supplemental material is mapped onto the test items in DTBS and redeveloped.
- **Conducting the DTBS tests.** In the sample schools, type A DTBS tests are administered in June, type B tests in September, and type C tests in December. The results of sampling are then used in test analysis, test equating, and other DASOBS activities.

The cut scores for test types A, B, and C are again uploaded to the database, and students who rank below-basic take the other types of DTBS tests and are provided with adjusted supplemental material.

DASOBS Results

Neither the diagnostic test nor the DTBS is mandatory; each metropolitan or provincial office of education may use the tests as it wishes. Some offices of education that decide to use the system print out the tests themselves and distribute the copies to schools, while others simply allows the schools print copies on their own.

Schools generally do not report to the MOE the percentage of students who place below-basic because they consider the DASOBS score reports as a formative evaluation for learning rather than a summative evaluation. Therefore, the exact number of students who have participated in the diagnostic test in March remains unknown. In recent years, however, offices of education have supported the use of DASOBS and suggested that the appropriate students be registered in the system for proper management. It seems that most schools use the initial diagnostic test to place students either below- or above-basic.

Students who place below-basic or are endorsed for DASOBS management by their teachers are registered in the system and must take the DTBS tests. **Table 4** shows the number of students who took the tests in 2015–2019, and the passing rate during the period is traced in a graph in **Figure 7**.

According to **Table 4**, the number of students who took the DTBS tests online during the period peaked in June and bottomed out in December. As shown in **Figure 7**, the passing rate was similarly at its lowest in June and at its highest in December.

Table 4: Number of Examinees for DTBS and Passing Rate (%)

Year	Number of DTBS examinees			Passing rate (%)		
	June	September	December	June	September	December
2015	225,922	186,622	156,429	56.58	62.69	65.48
2016	196,574	172,624	148,069	56.10	58.30	64.25
2017	181,224	158,104	144,942	54.67	57.37	62.93
2018	204,280	168,596	152,326	54.90	57.20	62.00
2019	173,103	136,845	132,722	58.00	61.20	64.80

DTBS = Diagnostic Test for Basic Skills.
Source: Korea Education and Research Information Service.

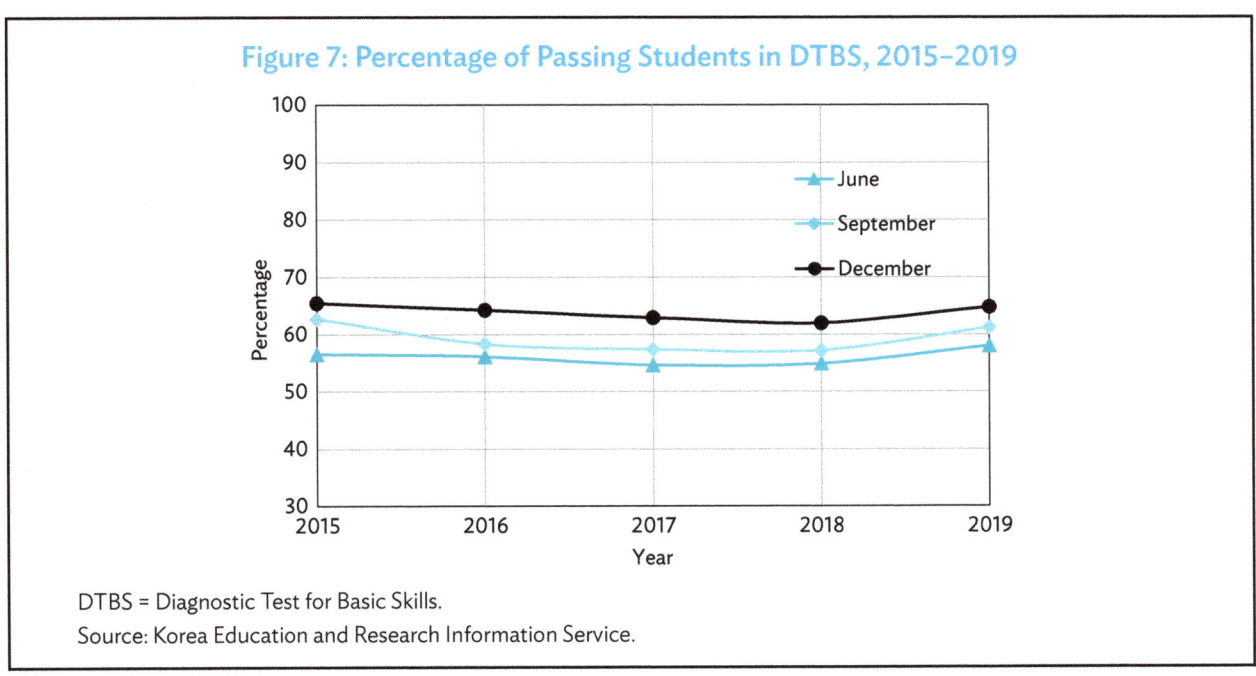

Figure 7: Percentage of Passing Students in DTBS, 2015–2019

DTBS = Diagnostic Test for Basic Skills.
Source: Korea Education and Research Information Service.

DASOBS advises schools to register below-basic learners in the system for management throughout the year. **Table 5** shows the number of schools that carried out the DTBS in 2019. DTBS is carried out in June, September, and December; 51.7%, 45.4%, and 46.5% of all registered elementary, middle, and high schools, respectively, used DTBS. The Government of the ROK directs its attention to elementary and middle schools, rather than high schools,

Table 5: Number of Schools that Conducted the DTBS in 2019

Item	School level	June (Test type A01)	September (Test types A02 and B01)	December (Test types A03, B02, and C01)
Number of registered schools	Elementary	6,468	6,460	6,884
	Middle	3,358	3,347	3,536
	High	2,144	2,146	2,263
	Subtotal	11,970	11,953	12,683
Number of schools that conducted DTBS	Elementary	4,047	3,623	4,033
	Middle	1,818	1,512	1,589
	High	327	296	273
	Subtotal	6,192	5,431	5,895
Percentage of schools that conducted DTBS	Elementary	62.57	56.08	58.59
	Middle	54.14	45.17	44.94
	High	15.25	13.79	12.06
	Subtotal	51.73	45.44	46.48

DTBS = Diagnostic Test for Basic Skills.
Source: Korea Education and Research Information Service.

when it comes to policies related to basic academic levels. Among the elementary and middle schools registered in DASOBS, 59.7% ran the DTBS in June 2019, 52.4% in September of that year, and 54% in December.

Table 6 shows the number of students who took the DTBS and the percentage of students who passed the tests in June, September, and December in 2019. The test in June is intended for students registered in the system who placed below-basic on the diagnostic test in March. The 173,103 DTBS examinees in June made up about 6.5% of the estimated 2,668,559 students from grades 4 to 9 in the registered schools (KERIS, 2019).

Among students who took the test in June 2019, 58% of them passed the test. The passing rate in September was 61.2%, while in December, it was 64.8%.

As may be expected, some students pass all the tests; however, others pass only type A, or none at all. Students who reach at least the standard in type A have been said to have made some progress in learning during the year. While students who do not pass a single test during the year can be regarded as having accumulated learning deficiencies over several years.

To use DASOBS properly, teachers must receive training in the system. Therefore, each office of education selects a certain number of teachers to go through a 2-day DASOBS training. In 2019, teachers who had received this training, and had used the system for 2 years, were surveyed. Of the 58 teachers in the survey, 75.86% affirmed (answered "strongly agree" or "agree") that the content of DASOBS is useful in diagnosing and guiding below-basic students, 75.87% said that they had a good knowledge of the content and its various types, 62.07% declared the content appropriate for learning, and 68.96% expressed general satisfaction with the DASOBS content.

Table 6: Number of Examinees and the Percentage of Those Passed in 2019 DTBS

School	No. of examinees and passing %	DTBS testing period		
		June	September	December
Elementary school	No. of examinees	104,900	86,560	85,405
	Passing %	61.51	66.55	70.02
Middle school	No. of examinees	68,203	50,285	47,317
	Passing %	52.66	52	55.35
Total	No. of examinees	173,103	136,845	132,722
	Passing %	58.02	61.2	64.79

DTBS = Diagnostic Test for Basic Skills.
Source: Korea Education and Research Information Service.

V. Implications for Policy Planning

Determining the percentage of below-basic students, on the basis of tests administered in sample schools, is important in education policymaking; however, finding out who these underachieving students are by giving the diagnostic test to all students, defining their levels of knowledge and comprehension, and providing below-basic students with proper and individualized support is much more important. DASOBS has several education policy implications in this regard.

First, the curriculum content taught in schools is hierarchical in structure and interrelated within and between grades. Teachers can greatly improve the academic success of students by ensuring that they move onto their next grade with the basic learning abilities from the current grades, especially if they start supporting students early in their school lives. There is a great need for an assessment system that continuously monitors students' achievement of learning goals from lower grades to higher ones. Allowing academically underachieving students to move up in grade and experience even more cases of school failure can exponentially magnify their discomfort in the classroom.

Second, after identifying academically underachieving students and their current level, schools must have a supplemental system in place that efficiently guides these students according to their grade and subjects, and continuously monitors them throughout the year. In all of this, the hardest part is not diagnosing underachievement, but steering the students toward studying by themselves. This is something schools must do on their own. The Do-Dream Schools, mentioned at the start of this report, help students who are likely to struggle in school because of their background (lack of motivation to learn, behavioral problems, emotional instability, learning disabilities, attention deficit disorder, inability to adjust to the current school, etc.), with various types of care provided by a multidisciplinary team.

There are about 2,900 Do-Dream Schools around the country. While DASOBS pays particular attention to the basic academic abilities of students, these schools focus on social-psychological problems in the school setting. The MOE also provides financial support with 17 metropolitan and provincial offices of education running Comprehensive Learning Clinic Centers (CCCL) set up specifically for supporting below-basic students with learning difficulties beyond the capacity of the schools to manage (MOE 2020).

Third, for DASOBS to operate as it should, there must be an entity specializing in its development and operation, or a control tower that organizes and oversees institutions and supports the administrative and financial part of the system, as is being done in the ROK. As stated earlier, several organizations in the country, including the MOE, metropolitan and provincial offices of education, a university with psychometric expertise, the management system for school internet networks nationwide, and schools, collaborate on the running of DASOBS. Efficient teamwork among the related institutions is required to provide all the things that DASOBS strives to offer.

Fourth, to equip teachers to give proper guidance to below-basic students, they must be trained in suitable teaching methods. Opportunities to share success stories can also be helpful. In addition, involving teachers in the item development process and setting of standards can make them understand students better and help students overcome the specific academic challenges they face. Teachers thus engaged can also share their experience or knowledge with their fellow teachers in their region.

Fifth, there must be an online system that enables below-basic students to regularly learn through items and learning material that match their level. This online system should allow students to diagnose their learning difficulties and supplement these on their own. Teachers can contribute by sharing their own content on this online platform. Posting videos and other content related to specific subject areas for students to use is important. Implementing a learning analysis system that suggests the next learning content, depending on what the students have been learning previously, is also something to consider.

Schwab (2016) pointed out that the Fourth Industrial Revolution will bring great changes to corporations and economies, thus worsening the economic inequalities that already exist. It is therefore more important than ever for countries to ensure that academically underachieving students can succeed in this new era. Guaranteeing that students gain the basic level of academic skills as a matter of policy is not a dispensation but a duty. All people are entitled to obtain the education needed to live and thrive in society through the public education system. Similarly, it is important to implement a high-quality education system that strives for equality in the education process.

No child wants to fall behind in school. Academically struggling students are so often isolated from the classroom simply because they learn differently. However, to achieve equality in classrooms, schools need to provide these students with an educational environment that welcomes them and truly cares for them. The real key to this is to make meaningful learning happen, even among the lowest-achieving students.

References

BASECAMP website. http://www.plasedu.org.

F. B. Baker and S.-H. Kim, eds. 2004. *Item Response Theory: Parameter Estimation Techniques*. 2nd ed. New York: Marcel Dekker, Inc.

G. J. Cizek, ed. 2012. *Setting Performance Standards: Foundations, Methods, and Innovations*. 2nd ed. New York: Routledge.

S. Kim et al. 2020. An Exploration of Patterns and Relationships among Below Basic Levels in Various Subjects of the 2016–2018 Diagnostic Tests of Basic Skills for Elementary Students. *Korean Journal of Educational Evaluation*. 33 (1). pp. 245–269.

M. J. Kolen and R. L. Brennan. 2014. *Test Equating, Scaling, and Linking: Methods and Practices*. 3rd ed. New York: Springer.

Korean Education and Research Information Service (KERIS), Republic of Korea. 2020. *The Completion Report of Year 2019 DASBOS Operation*. Report presented at the conference of Year 2019 DASBOS project. March.

Ministry of Education (MOE), Republic of Korea. 2016. *The 2017 Master Plan to Support for Improving the Basic Academic Ability of Students*. Press release. December.

———. 2019. *The Substantiality Plan to Support the Basic Academic Ability of Students for a Happy Starting*. Press release. March.

———. 2020. *The 2020 Plan to Support for Improving the Basic Academic Ability of Students*. Press release. 17 March.

H. C. Mitzel et al. 2001. The Bookmark Procedure: Psychological Perspectives. In G. J. Cizek, ed. *Setting Performance Standards: Concepts, Methods, and Perspectives*. Mahwah, NJ: Lawrence Erlbaum Associates. pp. 249–281.

Organisation for Economic Co-operation and Development (OECD). 2016. *Low-Performing Students: Why They Fall Behind and How to Help Them Succeed*. Programme for International Student Assessment (PISA). Paris: OECD Publishing. https://doi.org/10.1787/9789264250246-en

S. S. Ra, S. S. Kim, and K. J. Rhee. 2019. *Developing National Student Assessment Systems for Quality Education: Lessons from the Republic of Korea*. Manila: Asian Development Bank.

K. Schwab. 2016. *The Fourth Industrial Revolution*. Geneva: World Economic Forum.

About the Authors

Jae-Chun Ban is a professor at Chungnam National University in the Republic of Korea. He is also the director of the university's Applied Measurement and Evaluation Center responsible for developing the Diagnose-and-Supplement System of Basic Skills (DASOBS). As a psychometrician, he is interested in large-scale test development, item response theory, equating, standard setting, and cognitive diagnostic modeling.

Sun Kim is a research professor at Chungnam National University's Applied Measurement and Evaluation Center. She also plans, develops, and runs the DASOBS. She is also a psychometrician. Her areas of interest include large-scale and classroom test development, item response theory, equating, standard setting, feedback, and performance assessment as areas of particular interest.

Meekyung Shin is an education specialist from the Education Sector Group of the Sustainable Development and Climate Change Department at the Asian Development Bank. She collaborated with coauthors for this publication to help identify good practices in addressing the needs of lagging students.